# 365
# Housekeeping
# Tips

Text: Petra Sander
Translation: Kirsten Marxen
Copy Editing: APE Overath
Cover design: BOROS, Wuppertal
Cover photography (center) © Christel Rosenfeld

© 2000 DuMont monte UK, London

ISBN 3-7701-7005-9
Printed in Slovenia

# 1

## Bathing Caps

Swimming caps that are lightly
coated with glycerine and sprinkled
with talcum will not become
brittle, even through long
periods of disuse.

# General Topics

## Amber

To bring back the sparkle of amber, immerse it in methanol, wipe with a soft cloth, then polish it with a cloth soaked in cologne.

**3**

# Down Comforters

When the down in your comforter

begins to clump up, to make it snuggly

soft again, pick a small hole in the seam

and blow inside with a hair dryer

set on low.

**4**

# Bed Warmers

Because prune and cherry pits store heat for a long time, they make

excellent bed warmers when heated carefully and placed in bags.

# 5

## Twine

To make twine almost tear-proof, soak it in an alum solution.

# 6

## Glasses

Polish eyeglasses with glycerine and a chamois to keep them from fogging whenever you enter a heated room from the cold outdoors.

## 7 Brushes

New brushes last longer if you immerse them in a highly concentrated salt solution for a while.

## 8 Iron

Clean and care for your iron with a mixture of wood ash and vegetable oil.

# 9

## Earmarks

**Repair dog-eared pages in books by carefully dampening the creases and then ironing them on low.**

# 10

## Bicycle Spokes

Coating your bicycle spokes with clear petroleum

jelly prevents rust.

# 11

## Humidity

To minimise wood damage and mould growth due to humidity, place a bowl with a pound of quick-lime or calcium carbonate in each room (out of reach of pets and children) to absorb excess moisture. Change the quick-lime, or dry the calcium carbonate in a low oven, once in a while if the humidity persists.

# 12

## Slippery Soles

**Gluing a little bit of felt to your shoe soles can prevent slides on black ice in winter.**

# 13

## Gift Wraps

Creases in used gift wrap paper vanish if you iron the paper from
the opposite side. Adhesive tape can also be removed
more easily when warm.

## Glass Panes

To make glass panes opaque—in doors or windows, for example—coat
them with a mixture of half a pound of salt and one cup of very light beer.
The milky layer will wash off easily later.

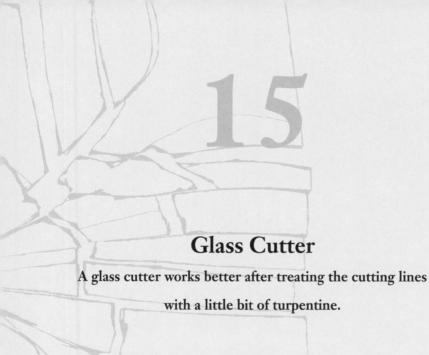

# 15

## Glass Cutter

A glass cutter works better after treating the cutting lines
with a little bit of turpentine.

# 16

## Cleaning Glass Vases

Clean dirt rings from your glass vases by filling them with a solution of detergent and letting them sit for a while. The ring will then wipe away easily.

## Gold

To clean gold, use warm water with a
dash of liquid ammonia added.

## Verdigris

Kerosene removes verdigris from brass without scratching the metal.

# 19

## Hammer

Pound an iron wedge into the top of the head of a
hammer to make the head very secure.

# 20

## Heating

Attach aluminium foil to the wall behind your radiator so that the heat reflects out into the room rather than being absorbed by the wall.

# 21

## Wood Screws

Wood screws screw into wood more easily if you roll them on a piece of dry soap, coating the threads.

## 22

### Fireplace Smells

**Cover the odour of dead ash in a cold fireplace by tossing dried flowers or berries into the fire just before it goes out.**

## 23

### Leaking Ceramic Vases

**Floor polish or varnish swished around inside leaky ceramic vases stops water seepage.**

# 24

Before inserting new candles into candlesticks, dip the lower ends of the candles into hot water just long enough to soften them for a snug, stable fit.

## Candle Rests

**25**

Immerse candlesticks in hot water
for a little while to easily remove
tough candle stubs.

**26**

## Dripping Candles

To prevent candles dripping,
soak them in salt water
for about an hour.

# 27

## Cleaning Baskets

The best, most gentle way to clean woven baskets is with a brush and warm salt water. Afterward, polish them with a soft cloth.

# 28

## Cork

To loosen a stubborn cork, warm the bottleneck
by rubbing it with a piece of cloth,
or hold a match to the bottleneck.

# 29

# Cleaning Crystal Vases

Get your crystal vases crystal clear again by shaking them vigorously

with water and pieces of orange peel inside.

# 30

## Ball Point Pens

Sometimes ballpoint pens stop writing even when the cartridge is still full.

Removing the cartridge and soaking it in warm water for a

short time gets ink flowing again.

# 31

## Copper Vases

Cut flowers keep longest in copper vases, because the metal releases antibacterial particles into the water. Achieve this effect in any vase by adding a copper penny to the flower water.

# 32

## Patent Leather Shoes

**To keep patent leather shoes from becoming brittle, treat them with vegetable oil once in a while and polish with a soft cloth when dry. A little castor oil will prevent the new patent leather from creasing.**

## 33

### Glue

Lightly beaten egg white can be used as glue. Onion juice also works, as long as both surfaces are first washed with soda water and dried thoroughly.

# 34

## Marble

**Lemon juice is an excellent stain remover for marble. Just be sure to clean it off very quickly, before citric acid damages the finish.**

## 35 Brass

Get your brass shining like new by polishing
it with a paste of salt and vinegar.

## 36 Opaque Glass

Hot vinegar water is the gentlest cleaner
for opaque glass.

# 37

## Large Nails

To hammer a large nail into a wall without the plaster crumbling,

warm the nail in hot water and then dip

the tip into vegetable oil.

# 38

## Pulling out Nails

To protect a wall when pulling out nails, slide a small piece of wood under the pliers. This also increases leverage, and the nail comes out more easily.

## 39

# Hammering Nails into Wood

Wood does not splinter when hammering in nails

if you dull the tip of the nail by hitting it with the hammer.

**40**

## Loose Nails

**Fix a loose nail by wrapping some cotton around it,
dipping it in glue and reinserting it into its hole.**

## Oil Paint

Leftover oil paint stays usable if you
drizzle some water on top to prevent
a skin from developing.

## Oil Paint and Brushes

Thoroughly clean paintbrushes used for oil paint in turpentine after use.
If they have dried out, soak them in hot, soapy water, then rinse well with
turpentine.

# 43

## Waterproofing Wrapping Paper

To waterproof wrapping paper, dip it into a mixture of one tablespoon grated beeswax, one tablespoon grated white soap, half a cup of alum solution and two cups of hot water. Let it dry.

## Grease Stains on Paper

Grease stains on paper disappear if you warm the paper
and then sprinkle some cornstarch onto the stain.
Brush off the dry starch with a soft brush.

# 45

## Inflammable Paper

**Paper soaked in a highly concentrated alum solution is fireproof.**

# 46

## Transparent Paper

**A thin coating of vegetable oil makes white paper transparent.**

## Kerosene Lamps

Adding a little turpentine and camphor to the kerosene in your lamp makes it burn brighter and use less fuel. A pinch of salt added also produces a brighter flame.

# 48

## Smoking Kerosene Lamps

To keep kerosene lamps from smoking, soak the wicks in vinegar
for a few hours and let them dry before use.

## Rust Protection

Instead of using chemical protection, metal can be treated with a mixture of three parts lard to one part resin.

## 50

## Sawing

Before sawing, cover the saw line with adhesive tape, then saw through the tape; the wood will not splinter. Drawing the blade edge through a dry piece of soap beforehand also makes for easier sawing.

# 51

## Sandals

Glue small strips of foam rubber to the insides of sandal straps, and they will not slip off your heel.

# 52

## Records

Wipe scratched vinyl records with a lint-free cloth moistened with machine oil, then enjoy them with no skipping.

# 53

## Matte Varnish

**To gently clean doors, doorframes and furniture coated with matte varnish, use unsalted potato cooking water.**

# 54

## Locks

**To open stuck locks, apply graphite to the movable parts.**

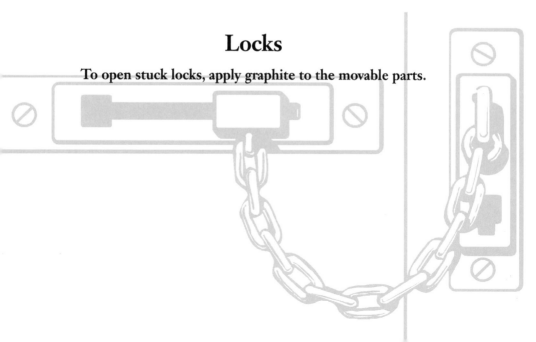

# 55

## Shoelaces

When you lose the tapes at the ends of shoelaces and the laces fray,
simply dip the ends into transparent nail polish to make them
pointed and stiff again.

## Unscrewing Screws

Loosen tight screws by heating
them with a soldering iron—the
hot metal of the screw expands
and enlarges the screw hole.
When the metal cools and
contracts, the screw is easily
removed.

# 57

## Drawers

**To prevent stubborn drawers from sticking, rub the sliding surfaces with a bit of soap.**

# 58

## Tight shoes

If shoes are too tight, swab their insides with alcohol and put the shoes on immediately. They will then stretch to fit your feet.

# 59

## Soles of Shoes

**Roughen slippery leather soles by rubbing them with fine sandpaper.**

# 60

## Shoulder Straps

**Foam rubber strips glued to the insides of shoulder straps keep them on your shoulder.**

# 61

## Sponges

Clean sponges by soaking them in a solution of a quarter pound of salt

and 4 cups of water for 24 hours.

**62**

## Soap Rests

Collect soap remnants, melt them and mix with some quartz sand.

The resulting solidified mass is effective in removing persistent stains

from your hands.

## Pins

Pick up dropped pins with a little magnet—it is a good way to ensure that you get them all.

# 64

## Hinges

A little graphite powder is a quick fix for squeaking doors—just sprinkle it on the moving parts of the hinges. The tip of a pencil works well, too.

# 65

## Moving

To move heavy furniture over flat surfaces more easily, place a piece of bacon rind, greasy side down, under the feet.

# 66

## Vases

Long twigs and flowers in arrangements are more stable if you affix

a piece of plastic foam to the inner rim of the vase.

## 67

## Cleaning Small Vases

To clean the inside of vases that are too small
to fit a cloth into, add a little soapy water and
uncooked rice, then shake vigorously.

# 68

## Christmas Trees

Help your Christmas tree keep its needles longer by adding glycerine to its water—two parts water to one part glycerine. Ideally, allow the tree to stand in the liquid for two days before the festivities.

# 69

## Suede Shoes

**Worn suede shoes can look as good as new if you roughen them with fine sandpaper and then buff them with a little vinegar.**

# In the Kitchen

## Smelly Sinks

Freshen smelly sinks by dissolving borax in hot water and pouring it down the drain. This also prevents greasy build-up in the plumbing. Baking soda can be used in the same way.

## 71

### Versatile Detergent

To make a cleaning solution effective on
almost any surface, heat two cups of vinegar
and add two or three drops of lavender oil.
You can also substitute rosemary oil,
if you prefer.

## Aluminium

Boiling the peels of three or more rhubarb

stalks in a tarnished aluminium pot will revive

its sparkle.

# 73

## Cookie Sheets

Easily remove tenacious crusty deposits from your cookie sheets by using crumpled newspaper to rub salt onto them. For rust stains, simply scrub salt into them with a bacon rind.

## Chrome

Clean dull chrome with turpentine
or kerosene, and then polish it
with a soft cloth. A paste of
whiting and vinegar works as well;
just rinse thoroughly,
then dry with a tea towel.

# 75

## Disinfecting

**Pure lavender oil is a natural disinfectant for all kitchen utensils and surfaces.**

# 76

## Stainless Steel

To get your stainless steel sink gleaming again, rub on a paste of whiting
and vinegar and let it sit for a while. Clean off the paste with a damp cloth,
and finish by polishing with a soft cloth. Any rust stains
can be rubbed off carefully with a little bit of benzene.

## Ivory

Wash ivory in lukewarm milk or soapy water, then polish it
with a soft cloth.

# 78

## Glasses

For spotless drinking glasses, wash them in hot, soapy water, then rinse them with cold salt water. When they are dry, polish them with a soft cotton cloth.

# 79

## Freezer

**Reduce ice build-up in your freezer by rubbing the interior with glycerine.**

**Any ice that does build up will detach much more easily when defrosting.**

# 80

## Electrical Burners

For regular care of electrical burners, wipe them with a few drops of machine oil. To clean them, turn burners on low and sponge them off with a dusting of baking powder. Cool, then rinse thoroughly with water.

# 81

## Horn

Clean horn handles on silverware under running water with a soft cloth, then rinse them off with a little liquid ammonia. After the handles dry, polish them with a small amount of vegetable oil.

# 82

## Cooking Utensils

To deodorise your cooking utensils
of fish, onion or cabbage smells, douse
them with hot water and some
white wine vinegar.

# 83

## Smells in the Refrigerator

**A saucer of baking soda placed in the fridge absorbs food odours.**

# 84

## Refrigerator Sealing Rubber

**An occasional light dusting of talcum powder on the rubber seal around your refrigerator door keeps it from becoming brittle and leaky.**

## Copper

To clean copper pots, use a solution of one part vinegar and one part salt.

Then rinse them thoroughly with water and polish with a soft cloth.

Wiping tarnished copper with the cut surface of half an onion is another

way to bring back its shine.

# 86

## Milk Pitchers

**If your milk pitcher starts to smell sour, rinse it out with a solution of baking soda dissolved in hot water.**

# 87

## Mother-of-Pearl

**To spruce up mother-of-pearl, apply a paste of whiting and water, let dry, then polish with a soft cloth.**

## Pans

Easily dissolve residue burnt onto pans by boiling a solution of one tablespoon of baking soda to four cups of water in those pans.

## Porcelain

Scrubbing porcelain with water and wheat germ is the best way to keep it clean. Then rinse the dishes with cold water and dry well. For burn stains on porcelain, scrub carefully with a cork dipped in salt, then rinse.

## Römertöpfe

Like all unglazed clay vessels, Römertopfe should be washed with hot
water only. The porous material absorbs any detergent used and
releases it into foods cooked in the pot later.

# 91

## Silver

To brighten your silver, try this: Fill a plastic bowl with hot water and place a piece of aluminium foil in it. Dissolve a teaspoon of salt and a teaspoon of baking soda in the water, then wrap the silver item in the foil. When it becomes shiny, any residual coating can easily be removed with a soft cloth.

# 92

## Silver

Keep silver from tarnishing by storing it in a dark place wrapped in plastic bags, or by wiping it now and then with a little bit of olive oil.

# 93

## Dishwashing Detergent

A drop of herbal vinegar in the dishwater gets greasy dishes squeaky-clean—just be sure to rinse thoroughly afterward with clear water. A solution made from leftover pieces of soap dissolved in hot water with a splash of borax is also excellent for dishwashing.

## Teapots

To brew truly fragrant tea, rinse your teapots only
with clear water—residual tannins in the teapot
enhance tea's flavour. If you do want to remove the
residue, soak the pot in vinegar or lemon juice
and rinse thoroughly several times with water.

# 95

## Kettles

Dissolve lime build-up in water kettles by boiling a mixture of one part water and one part vinegar in them. Let the liquid rest in the pot for a few hours, then rinse thoroughly with water.

# 96

## Zinc

Strong soda water makes zinc cups sparkle. Just boil some soda water, immerse the cups in it briefly, then rinse them off with hot water.

**97**

## Preventing Burnt Milk

If you add a tablespoon of sugar to hot milk, it cannot burn. You can also boil milk in a pot with water sprinkled on the inside.

# Kitchen Secrets

# 98

## Apples

**Submerging apples in hot water for a minute makes it easier to peel them.**

# 99

## Blanching

To keep vegetables fresh and bright when blanching, simply add a
teaspoon of baking soda to the water.

# 100

## Cauliflower

A drop of vinegar added to the cooking water helps cauliflower maintain its creamy white colour. A few of the green leaves in the water intensifies this vegetable's often mild flavour.

## Frying Fat

**A pinch of salt keeps frying fat from splattering out of the pan.**

# 101

# 102

## Fried Potatoes

**For really crisp fried potatoes, roll the pieces in flour before frying them.**

# 103

## Sausages

Roll sausages in a little bit of flour before frying to make them wonderfully crisp.

# 104

## Bread

Before cutting very fresh bread, warm the bread knife so that the soft bread won't stick to it. To prevent fresh bread from becoming mouldy, store it in a used flour sack and hang it in a dry basement.

# 105

## Bread

To revive stale bread, place it in a clay dish, cover it with a lid and set the clay dish in hot water.

# 106

## Butter

Add a dash of vegetable oil to butter so that it doesn't darken during frying. To make rancid butter good as new, first melt it and skim off the foam. Then add a toasted piece of black bread crust to the hot butter. Remove the crust after 15 minutes, and the butter is ready to be used.

## Eggs

To test the age of an egg, immerse it
in a solution of 1/2 cup of salt to 4
cups of water. If it sinks, the egg is
fresh; if it goes down only half way, it
is one or two days old. It the egg is
more than three days old, it will float.
Coating eggs in linseed oil keeps
them fresh longer.

# 108

## Ice Makers

To keep conventional ice makers from freezing to the bottom of the freezer compartment, wipe the bottom of the dish with a little vegetable oil.

# 109

## Peas

**Peas stay bright green when you add a pinch of sugar to the boiling water.**

# 110

## Pea Soup

A piece of bread added to pea soup will keep the peas from sticking to the bottom of the pot and burning.

**111**

## Vinegar

A simple recipe for homemade vinegar is to mix 4 cups of wine, 4 cups of

distilled water and a scant cup of diced fresh black bread crust in a bottle.

Close the bottle and leave it in a warm spot.

The vinegar will be ready in a week.

# 112

## Fish

To easily scale whole fish without damaging the tender meat, first immerse the fish briefly in hot water, then immediately afterward in cold.

# 113

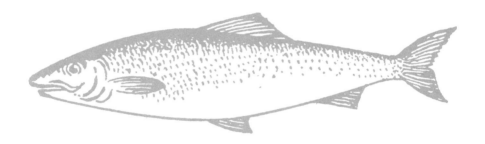

## Fresh Fish

If you press a fish with your fingertip and the impression remains visible,

the fish is less than fresh. The faster the indentation disappears,

the fresher the fish.

# 114

## Fish Smells

**Lemon juice removes fish odours from hands and dishes.**

# 115

## Bottles

It is easy to open screw-top bottles containing non-carbonated liquids if you first turn the bottle upside down and hit the bottom with the flat of your hand.

# 116

## Meat

Retain the full nutritive value of meat by immersing it in hot water or hot fat. This closes the cells that are opened by cutting, and seals in both the meat's nutrients and its juices.

# 117

## Vegetables

Root vegetables are best cooked in a lidded pot; vegetables grown above
ground can cook without a lid.

# 118

## Salting vegetables

**To help vegetables retain their full nutritive value when boiling, save the salt until just before they are done.**

# 119

## Vegetable Stains

Remove vegetable stains from your fingers by rubbing them with a slice of raw potato or lemon.

# 120

## Grog

Prevent hot drinks from cracking your glasses simply by placing a spoon in the glass, then pouring the liquid onto the spoon.

# 121

## Legumes

Ward off some of the less pleasant (digestive) side effects of eating
legumes—peas, beans, lentils and such—by adding 1/4 teaspoon
baking soda per cup of cooking water.

# 122

## Cheese

**Soak dried-out cheese in milk for a little while to restore its freshness.**

# 123

## Grating Cheese

**Ripe, hard cheeses are best for dishes that call for a topping of melted cheese because young cheeses are hard to grate.**

# 124

## Preparing Potatoes

Adding a little margarine to the cooking water helps potatoes cook faster.

# 125

## Peeling Potatoes

Peeling older, shrivelled potatoes is easier when they have been soaked in cold water. Peeled potatoes will keep in the refrigerator for several days without turning brown if they are stored in a bowl of water with a few drops of vinegar added.

# 126

## Dumplings

**Revive day-old dumplings by putting them into cold water and reheating them. When the dumplings rise to the surface, they are ready.**

## Cabbage

Cooking odours from cabbage can be strong. Adding a teaspoon of baking soda to the cooking water can alleviate that, and helps the cabbage soften faster, as well. With red cabbage, use a dash of vinegar for the same effect.

# 128

## Swiss Chard

To weed out the woody parts of Swiss chard before they make their way onto your dinner plate, boil the chard whole and only then cut it into pieces. The parts that have remained tough are then easy to sort out.

# 129

## Cakes

If a cake sticks to the pan after baking, place the pan on a cold, wet tea towel for a few minutes.

## Cake Dough

To keep nuts and raisins from sinking to the bottom of the cake dough, rinse them briefly in water and then dust them with flour. A few drops of vinegar will make the dough even lighter.

# 131

## Graters

**Sharpen dull graters by rubbing them with sandpaper.**

# 132

## Carrots

Carrots are cut most easily at room temperature, so remove them from the refrigerator an hour before they are needed.

# 133

## Natural Sponges

**Natural sponges kept in the refrigerator's vegetable crisper soak up humidity, keeping vegetables nice and fresh.**

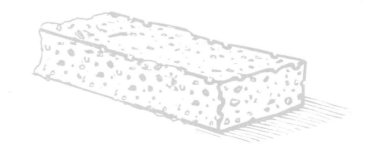

## Washing Fruit

To get fruits really clean, dissolve a little baking soda in the washing water.

# 135

## Pepper

Ground pepper in a pepper shaker stays fresh and aromatic longer when you add a few kernels of whole pepper.

# 136

## Pudding

Not everyone likes the skin that develops on homemade puddings. Sprinkling a little sugar onto the pudding while it is still warm helps it cool without developing a skin.

# 137

## Rice

For especially white rice, add a little lemon juice to the cooking water.

# 138

## Salting Steaks and Liver

**For maximum tenderness, don't salt beef steaks or liver until they are on the serving plate.**

# 139

## Fried Onions

**For crispy fried onions, sprinkle them with a little flour before frying.**

# 140

## Salt

**Keep salt in a salt shaker dry by adding a few grains of uncooked rice to it.**

# 141

## Sauerkraut and Potatoes

Never cut potatoes into sauerkraut, but cook them in separate pots.

Sauerkraut keeps potatoes from cooking thoroughly.

# 142

## Mould

**A little bit of lavender water added to bread dough keeps homemade bread from moulding.**

## Grilling Meat

**When grilling food outside, toss a few herbs directly onto the hot coals.**

**To help the herbed smoke permeate the meat, make a loose tent of**

**aluminium foil over the grill.**

# 144

## Whipped Cream

Adding a few drops of lemon juice to whipping cream helps it stiffen quickly and reliably. For especially fluffy whipped cream, add the white of a very fresh egg.

# 145

## Lids

Easily open tight jar lids by turning the jar upside down and hitting the bottom of the glass. You can also push small holes into the lid with the sharp point of a can opener. As soon as the vacuum is broken, the lid comes off easily.

## Sparkling Wine

Keep the sparkle in an open bottle of sparkling wine for several hours by inserting a teaspoon, handle first, into the bottle.

# 147

## Thickening Sauce

When using flour to thicken sauce, adding a little salt to the flour keeps it from clumping.

# 148

## Dark Sauces

**A pinch of sugar makes a dark sauce velvety smooth.**

# 149

## Peeling Tomatoes

If you briefly immerse tomatoes in boiling water before peeling them,

the skin comes away easily.

# 150

## Sponge Cake

When preparing a sponge cake with a fruit topping, spreading a thin layer of heated apricot jelly on the cake bottom prevents the fruit juices from soaking through and making the sponge cake soggy.

# 151

## Cutting Fancy Layered Cakes

**For clean cutting of torte or other fancy layered cakes, warm the knife beforehand in hot water.**

# 152

## Tubes

Hard-to-open tubes unscrew easily when
you hold the tube under hot water.

# 153

## Preventing Boiling Over

To keep milk from boiling over, lightly butter the inside rim of the pot.

# 154

## Oversalting

Save oversalted dishes simply by placing a small, clean sponge into the pot for a few minutes to absorb some of the salt. If necessary, thoroughly rinse the sponge and repeat. Another way to remove excess salt is to stretch a cloth napkin over the pot and place a handful of flour on it.

# 155

## Citrus Fruits

Oranges and lemons are easier to juice after having been rolled a few times on a hard surface.

# 156

## Peeling Onions

Briefly dipping an onion in lukewarm water before cutting it makes for fewer tears, and the skin comes off more easily. Cutting up the onion in a bowl of water brings no tears at all.

# Bathroom Hints

## 157

### Fittings

Eliminate lime stains from sink
and bath fittings with a little bit of
vinegar on a damp cloth—they
will sparkle like new.

# 158

## Bathtubs

A paste of borax and vinegar removes rust stains from dripping faucets in the tub. Apply the paste to the stain, leave it on for some time, then rinse thoroughly.

# 159

## Shower Heads

Vinegar and salt make the best cleaning agent for lime build-up on shower heads. Leave the solution on for a while, until the lime dissolves, then rinse quickly.

# 160

## Shower Curtains

Remove mould from your shower curtain by wiping it down with baking soda dissolved in lemon juice. Then soak the curtain in salt water for an hour, and rinse well.

# 161

## Tile Detergent

**A little vinegar on a damp cloth easily cleans lime stains on tiles.**

# 162

## Cleaning between the Tiles

**The grout between your bathroom tiles regains its gleaming whiteness when treated with whiting.**

# 163

## Hair Brushes

Clean hairbrushes approximately every two weeks in
a solution of 1/3 cup vinegar and 1 1/2 cups
lukewarm salt water. Thoroughly rinse the brushes
in water with a few drops of rosemary oil added,
and let them dry in the sun.

# 164

## Tiles

A cut lemon is an excellent cleaner for stained tiles. To restore their shine afterward, rub the tiles with a mixture of water and milk, rinse well, and then polish the tiles with a soft cloth.

# 165

## Nail Brush

**To clean your nail brush, soak it in cold vinegar water for several hours.**

# 166

## Nail Files

Clean your dirty nail file by sticking adhesive tape onto it. When you pull off the tape, the dirt comes with it.

# 167

## Natural Stone Tiles

Instead of glazing, you can waterproof natural stone tiles with linseed oil.

Let the oil soak in for at least two weeks before mopping the floor

for the first time.

# 168

## Mirrors

When your mirrors are steamy, wipe them off with warm water to which you have added a dash of both methanol and liquid ammonia.

# 169

## Toilet Bowls

Lime build-up in toilet bowls is best tackled with a paste of vinegar and flour. Spread the paste in the bowl and leave it on overnight. The next morning brush it off and rinse well.

# Ceilings, Walls and Floors

# 170

## Concrete Floors

Unsealed concrete floors—in the basement, for instance—should never be washed with soap but only damp-mopped, because the porous floor can absorb the soap.

# 171

## Picture Frames

Keep the pictures hanging on your walls from shifting by gluing bits of foam rubber to the back of the frame.

# 172

## Paste

For a completely environmentally safe wallpaper paste, stir one part rye or wheat flour into 15 parts boiling water.

# 173

## Laminated Floors

After mopping your laminated floors, dry them to prevent swelling due to any water that seeps through.

## Paint Smells

To take the edge off unpleasant paint fume odours, set plates with salt and onion halves around the room.

## Parquet

A pencil eraser easily erases dark stripes from parquet. Clear shoe polish also does the job. Treat more obstinate stains briefly with methanol, then remove thoroughly with warm water.

# 176

## PVC Floors, Linoleum Floors

Heel marks on PVC or linoleum floors remove easily with the rough side of a little dishwashing sponge. Steel wool soaked in methanol works well for tougher stains.

# 177

## Mould Stains

To eliminate mould stains on walls and ceilings, brush them with vinegar

water, blow-dry the spots with a hair dryer, and repeat until

the spots are gone.

# 178

## Cobwebs

Easily remove cobwebs from ceilings and walls with a broom wrapped in a damp cloth.

## Wall Painting

When painting your walls, insert just a little more than half the brush into the paint. This keeps the coating even, makes for an easier job at cleaning time, and preserves the brushes.

# 180

## Wallpapering

In wallpapering, it is best to apply paste to both the paper and the wall, especially when using heavy wallpaper. Creases and blisters brush away much more easily when the paste is wet and, when it is dry, the paper sticks better. Also, gluing pieces of aluminium foil over damp spots on walls before wallpapering keeps the paper from detaching later.

# 181

## Stains on Wallpaper

Treat grease stains on wallpaper with a paste of cornstarch and a little water. Let the paste dry, then brush it off carefully with a soft brush.

Grease spots can also be dabbed with cotton soaked in benzene.

A piece of bread crust is a gentle way to wipe away soot.

# 182

## Holes in Wallpaper

If you want to hammer a nail into a wall without leaving a hole in the wallpaper, use a sharp carpet knife to cut a little cross into the paper over where the hole will be, fold open the corners, and hammer in your nail. When you remove the nail later on, simply fold the corners closed.

# 183

## Blood Stains on Carpet

To clean a fresh blood stain on a carpet, pour carbonated mineral water onto it and then soak it up immediately with paper toweling. Repeat several times until the stain disappears.

## Fresh Carpet Colours

To revive the colours of your carpet, wipe the carpet with a cloth soaked in a solution of one part vinegar to three parts warm water.

# 185

## Grease Stains on Carpet

To remove a grease stain from a carpet, generously sprinkle flour onto the stain, leave it on for a while, then vacuum.

# 186

## Red Wine Stains on Carpet

Clean red wine stains from carpet by generously sprinkling salt onto the stains; leave it on for some time before you vacuum it off. Older stains should be moistened with cold water before starting the salt treatment.

# 187

## Soot Stains on Carpet

To remove soot from carpet, place a piece of newspaper next to the stain and use a bicycle pump to blow any loose soot onto the newspaper. Sprinkle a mixture of wheat bran and salt onto the rest, and brush it off with a stiff brush.

# 188

## Burn Stains on Carpet

To remove small burns from carpet, rub the marks with the
cut surface of half an onion.

# 189

## Carpet Corners Standing Out

Curled carpet corners are both unattractive and a hazard. To flatten them, spread cornstarch paste on the underside of the corners. When it has dried, iron the corners flat, placing a piece of paper between the iron and the carpet. Brush away residual starch with a nail brush.

# 190

## Moth Repellent

Sprinkling carpets occasionally with a little lavender oil keeps moths away.

## Putty

**Turpentine easily removes stains from window putty.**

# 191

# Windows and Curtain Care

# 192

## Chamois

To keep chamois soft after drying, wash it out with lukewarm water in which a little bit of salt has been dissolved.

# 193

## Window Cleaner

Wash windows with one part white vinegar and two parts water, then polish them with newspaper to get them squeaky clean with no streaking. Potato skins that have been washed in boiling water are also an excellent window cleaner—just wipe your windows with them, then polish with a soft cloth.

# 194

## Fly Droppings

Use black tea to wipe away fly dirt on windowsills.

## Curtain Pleats

After hanging newly washed curtains, create pleats by folding as desired

and then attaching clothespins to both the front and back of the curtains.

Remove the clothespins when the curtains are dry, and the pleats will

remain in place.

## Washing Curtains

To wash curtains without a washing machine, soak them in a solution of

one pound baking soda and two and one half gallons of water,

then rinse thoroughly.

# 197

## White Curtains

To make your white curtains snowy again, add a package of baking powder and a dash of both vinegar and lemon juice to the fabric softener compartment of your washing machine.

# 198

## Curtain Rods

A little talcum on the curtain rod helps curtains open and close much more easily.

# 199

## Dark Furniture

Maintain dark furniture with a mixture of one part vegetable oil to one part red wine.

## Furniture

## Oak Furniture Care

A furniture polish particularly suited to caring for oak includes a piece of beeswax, a tablespoon of fine sugar, one egg and a cup of water. Boil the mixture and let it cool completely, then apply it with a paint brush. When it has dried, polish the wood with a soft cloth.

# 201

## Fresh Colours

Brighten your upholstery with a solution of warm water, a pinch of salt and a dash of vinegar.

# 202

## Dog and Cat Hair

Use a damp sponge to clean animal hair off upholstery.

## Wood Care

Clean and maintain your furniture—and even make small scratches

disappear—by wiping it with a mixture of one part vinegar and one part

vegetable oil.

# 204

## Woodworms

Protect your furniture from woodworms with either a mixture of three drops of tea tree oil, one cup each of turpentine and vinegar, and two cups of boiled and cooled linseed oil. Apply a thin coating, then polish immediately.

# 205

## Leather Furniture

For the care of leather furniture, sponge on a mix of half a cup of water, half a cup of milk and one egg-white. When it has dried, buff the surfaces with a soft brush.

# 206

## Furniture Polish

A pinch of salt dissolved in a cup of vegetable oil is the simplest furniture polish of all.

# 207

## Cleaning Upholstery

To clean upholstery, sprinkle wheat bran onto it and massage it into the fabric with a cloth. Then simply brush off the bran, which lifts away the dirt. To dust upholstery, put a damp cloth over it, then beat it with an old tennis racket. The cloth catches the dust.

# 208

## Scratches on Furniture

**A little vegetable oil is effective for small scratches on wood furniture.**

# 209

## Untreated Wood

To make a protective coating for untreated wood, melt one cup of beeswax by placing in a heat-resistant bowl over a pot of hot (not boiling) water. Remove the melted wax from the heat and stir in one cup of turpentine oil, then let the mixture cool. Apply sparingly with a soft cloth, then polish with a clean cloth.

# Vermin

## Ants in the Kitchen

To make ants steer clear of your kitchen shelves, put out peppermint leaves, chillies or cloves. Wormwood, gentian or a saucer with a little kerosene will also drive ants away.

**210**

# 211

## Repelling Ants

Keep ants away from honey and sweets by drawing a thick line of chalk around the jars. Another way to protect food from ants is to place the feet of the table where the food is set out into filled water bowls.

# 212

## Killing Ants

If an ant colony makes its home in yours, a paste made of honey and yeast can eliminate it. Place bowls with one part yeast and two parts honey near the ant trails—the honey will attract the ants, and they will eat the yeast with it, feeding it in turn to their offspring. Yeast is poisonous for ants.

# 213

## Vermin in Dried Fruits

Immediately throw infested dried fruit into a bin outside the house.
Use vinegar water to thoroughly clean the kitchen cabinet where
the fruit was kept.

# 214

## Aphids

Cigarette or cigar ash is potent against aphids. Simply sprinkle the ashes onto the garden soil until the aphids have vanished.

# 215

## Aphids on Roses

In case of a mild infestation, simply dust aphids off the stems of roses with a small paintbrush. For heavier infestations, the best remedy is ladybugs. Release as many as possible onto the flowers.

# 216

## Horseflies

Washing with parsley tea makes you safe from bothersome horseflies. Washing with laurel leaf tea and garlic, or simply applying margarine to your skin, also keeps them away.

## White Grubs

To rid your flowerbeds of white grubs, sprinkle chalk onto the soil and rake it in a little bit.

**217**

## Sand Flies

**218**

These pests in the garden soil of your flowerpots will vanish if you stick a match head down into the dirt.

# 219

## Fruit Flies

A few drops of lavender oil in a small oil lamp repels fruit flies, as do lemons studded with a few whole cloves.

# 220

## Repelling Flies

To repel flies, hang up bundles of elder or
other potent herbs. To keep most types of flies
from entering the house, put pots of basil on
your windowsills.

## Fleas

Fleas will leave your dogs and cats alone if you tuck a little eucalyptus into their bedding. Some tea tree oil dabbed on the animal's collar also helps keep the parasites away.

# 222

## Freezing Pests

Freezing infested fabrics is an effective way to get rid of many kinds of insects. On very cold winter days you can rid whole carpets of vermin by leaving them in the garden or on the balcony.

# 223

## Cereal Pests

Repel insects from flour or cereal stores by adding a few bay leaves to them.

# 224

## Rabbits

To keep rabbits out of fruit or vegetable gardens, soak string in kerosene for a couple of hours and then surround the beds with it. Protect young trees by tying straw to their trunks up to a height of about three feet.

225

## Mites

The best protection against dust mites is to do without dust collectors like
carpets, upholstery, and curtains entirely. Towels and bedding are also
preferred locations, since dust mites feed on small pieces of skin. Airing
your towels and sheets in the sun has a disinfecting effect.

# 226

## Wood Worms

Spraying benzene or wormwood extract into wood worm holes helps repel these pests. They can also be lured out of wood into freshly peeled acorns placed in front of their holes, and then easily disposed of.

# 227

## Centipedes

If you have centipedes in your basement, lay out a damp rug overnight. The insects are attracted to it and can be carried outside with it in the morning.

# 228

## Cats

To protect birds' nests against cats, make a ring of long-necked plastic bottles, narrow end up with no space between them, and tie the ring around the tree about six feet from the ground.

# 229

## Wood lice

Put some boiled potatoes into empty flowerpots, cover the potatoes with wilted grass, and lean the pots against a basement wall (so the bugs can more easily crawl inside). Wood lice are drawn to the flowerpots and can then be removed easily.

## 230 Cherry Flies

To protect your cherries against cherry flies, attach yellow plastic covered with glue or another sticky substance to your trees as the fruit begins to ripen.

## 231 Cabbage Flies

A handful of wood ash sprinkled in the centre whorl of the young cabbage plant, just after cabbage flies appear, protects your harvest against cabbage fly larvae.

# 232

## Head Lice

An effective remedy against head lice is to wash scalp and hair (ideally short) with hot vinegar. Rubbing one's scalp with rosemary oil also helps against lice.

# 233

## Herbs

The essential oils of some herbs act as natural insect repellents. Basil, chervil, rosemary, peppermint and lemon balm are especially effective. You can also leave dried herbs on your windowsill.

# 234

## Moles

Evict moles from your lawn by soaking an old piece of cloth in kerosene, inserting the cloth into the mole's hole, and sealing the hole with dirt. For the same effect, the cloth can also be soaked in herring brine instead.

# 235

## Mice

Mice avoid peppermint, chilies, and cloves and can thus be kept at bay without mousetraps even by people who do not own a cat. Oleander leaves ground into powder and sprinkled into mouse holes also drives away mice.

## Moths

Moths stay away from wool if you place wormwood between the layers. Drive moths out of upholstery with vinegar steam: Simply cover your furniture with cloths, then put a hot tin bowl under the furniture and pour in a little vinegar. Since moths also dislike printing ink, newspaper tucked between layers and under cushions will keep them away—just replace it at least once a month.

236

# 237

## Mosquitoes

Repel mosquitoes with a few drops of laurel oil in small bowls or small oil lamps. Castor-oil plants (Ricinus communis) also keep mosquitoes away, so one plant in each room will keep your home mosquito-free. An effective mixture to apply to your skin is half a cup of almond oil or olive oil blended with 40 drops of lemon or clove oil.

# 238

## Fruit maggots

Draw fruit maggots out of fruit trees by belting the tree trunks with corrugated cardboard. When the larvae have collected in the ridges, remove and destroy the cardboard and the maggots with it.

## Earwigs

Since earwigs like to crawl into dark cracks and small gaps, catch them easily with some excelsior placed under a drinking glass in the evening. The next morning, slide a piece of paper under the glass and carry the earwigs outside.

# 240

## Small Oil Lamps

A few drops of essential oil added to a small oil lamp is an excellent remedy against insects that is of use both in the garden and on windowsills. Especially effective, for example, are lemon, peppermint, lavender and eucalyptus oils.

# 241

## Parquet Infestation

When a parquet floor is infested, there is unfortunately nothing to do but replace the wood. In winter, however, furniture and other wooden things can be carried outside; frost kills the larvae.

# 242

## Fur Pests

Throw out furs infested with bugs. Clothing where infestation is not obvious but may be a threat can be frozen for three days, then washed. Washing out the closet with a solution of vinegar water will keep it free of pests for a long time.

**243**

## Rats

Rats never stay long where guinea fowl is kept. Putting out valerian root also drives away rats, as do pieces of cloth soaked in kerosene and stuffed into rat holes and sealed in with dirt. Because rats may harbour dangerous diseases, call in professional pest control for a significant infestation.

# 244

## Caterpillars

**Protect cabbage from caterpillars by interplanting them with hemp plants (Cannabis sativa).**

# 245

## Cockroaches

Cockroaches avoid the smell of salted herring and can be driven out if you lay out several salted herrings in the infested rooms. For a heavy infestation, call in professional pest control, because cockroaches can transmit dangerous diseases.

# 246

## Scale Insects

Easily remove scale insects from an infested plant with a needle.

Afterward, wash the leaves of the plant with soapy water.

# 247

## Slugs

Since slugs prefer smooth surfaces, sprinkling a ring of sand around your flowerbeds will keep them away. Or catch the slugs in a beer trap: Sink a cup of beer into the ground next to the endangered flowerbed—the slugs fall into the cup and can be removed easily.

# 248

## Silverfish

**Evict silverfish from their hiding places by dabbing some diluted lavender oil in those spots.**

# 249

## Spider Mites

To eliminate spider mites, wash affected leaves repeatedly with mild soapy water until the mites have completely disappeared.

# 250

## Book Lice

Book lice like a lot of humidity, so a dry environment is the safest way to protect against them. Protect your books, wallpaper and food by regularly airing and, in winter, thoroughly heating your home.

# 251

## Bedbugs

Spraying acetic acid around the room and into the joints and corners of bed frames is infallible against bedbugs. Kerosene and turpentine oil are poisonous for bedbugs, but should only be applied in well-aired rooms.

# 252

## Wasps

To keep wasps out of the house, hang branches of stinging nettles in the windows. Draw wasps away from food outdoors by setting a glass half-filled with jam dissolved in wasser nearby, but out of the way. The smell of sautéed onions or steaming vinegar water also keeps wasps away.

# 253

## Wooly Aphids

If you wash plants infested with wooly aphids regularly with soapy water,
the pests will disappear.

# 254

## Voles

Protect plants against voles for a couple of years by wrapping the root balls in wire netting before planting. Drive away the uninvited guests with pieces of cloth soaked in kerosene and stuffed into their holes.

# 255

## Ticks

To remove ticks, rotate them for a while—whether clockwise or counter-clockwise is unimportant—and then remove them. Don't use oil or alcohol to try to kill ticks that have bitten you, because this causes them to inject more of their infectious saliva.

# Care of Clothing

**256**

## Angora

Wash angora clothing in lukewarm suds of gentle detergent and rinse it several times in tepid water, adding a little glycerine to the last rinse. Press the garment between two towels—do not wring. When it is dry, use a soft brush to restore its fuzziness. To prevent angora clothing from shedding, place it in a plastic bag and freeze it overnight.

# 257

## Patching Cotton

Repair holes in cotton clothing without lifting a needle by soaking a small
piece of cloth in dissolved cornstarch and ironing it onto the tear.

# 258

## Ironing Boards

If you cover your ironing board with a piece of silver foil, your laundry will almost iron itself. The foil reflects the heat and more or less irons the clothing from underneath.

# 259

## Clothing Irons

If you rub your hot iron with a candle and then wipe it off with a cloth, the iron will glide over your laundry more easily. Use only distilled water in your steam iron to prevent lime deposits in the nozzles, which can cause stains or even clog the nozzles completely.

# 260

## Pleats

To make pleats more crisp, wet the inside
of the fabric before ironing.

# 261

## Ironing

To prevent damage to delicate fabrics from ironing, place a thin tissue between the fabric and the iron. Black clothing is best ironed inside out because heat may damage the black pigment, resulting in irregularities in the garment's colour.

# 262

## Elastic Bands

Worn-out elastic waistbands or sleeve cuffs can be brought back into shape with a rubber thread pulled through the stitches with a darning needle.

# 263

## Pantyhose

Pantyhose regain their sheen when you rinse them in vinegar water after washing. To prevent striping, always hang socks and hosiery by the toes to dry.

# 264

## Blankets

Blankets will not lose their shape if they are hung, folded in triangles, after washing.

# 265

## Dark Fabrics

Boil one quarter cup of ivy leaves in four cups of water for five minutes and wash dark fabrics in the cooled (but not cold) extract—they will be as good as new.

# 266

## Thread

**Thread needles is easier while holding the eye against a contrasting background, dark for a pale thread and white for a dark thread.**

## Glowing Colours

Revive colourful fabrics by rinsing them in vinegar water before washing.

Never hang coloured fabrics in direct sunshine, which would bleach

out the colours.

# 268

## Felt

**Remove water stains from felt simply by roughing the fabric carefully with fine sandpaper.**

# 269

## Kid Gloves

**A little bit of glycerine applied to kid gloves keeps them soft.**

# 270

## Elastic Waistbands

**To replace worn-out elastic waistbands, attach one end of the old elastic to the new one with a safety pin. When you pull out the old elastic, you insert the new one at the same time.**

# 271

## Towels

Towels that have become rough regain their softness when boiled in salt water. Rinse well with plain water.

## Pants

Sewing a piece of silk to the insides of the knees of pants keeps the knees from going baggy with wear. The silk should be a little narrower than the inside of the pants from seam to seam.

272

273

## Pants Hangers

Glue a little piece of foam rubber to the insides of pants hangers to keep pants from sliding off.

# 274

## Jeans

To revive the colour of old jeans, wash them with a new pair.

# 275

## Clothes Hangers

**Rubber bands wrapped around the ends of clothes hangers keep blouses and shirts from slipping off.**

# 276

## Nicely Perfumed Closets

To infuse your closet—and thereby your clothes—with the scent of your favourite perfume, cut a piece of blotting paper into pieces and drizzle a few drops of perfume onto each. Distribute the paper around your closet.

# 277

## Moth Protection in your Closet

Lavender protects against moths and other insects.

Simply hang small lavender sachets over the

clothes rack and tuck additional sachets into

lingerie compartments.

# 278

## Knee Socks

To keep knee socks knee-high, simply turn down the top of the sock and hem it, then pull through an elastic band that fits your calf.

## Creases

Creases in jackets and pants disappear if you dampen the creased areas
and then hang up the garment. Steam works even faster for some fabrics;
hold the creased garment over a boiling kettle or even over hot, running
water from the bathtub faucet.

# 280

## Buttons

**Buttons stay well attached if you pull the thread through beeswax before sewing on the button.**

## 281

### Buttonholes

Buttonholes fray with time. To help
the opening regain its form, treat the
inside of the buttonhole with a few
drops of transparent nail polish.

## 282

### Rayon

Rinse rayon clothing in vinegar water after
washing to make it shinier.

# 283

## Leather

Care for leather garments by wiping them with castor oil
every two weeks.

# 284

## Coat Collars

The collar often gets dirtier faster than the rest of a coat. For interim cleanings, generously sprinkle the collar with baking powder and leave it on for one hour. Then simply brush off the baking powder.

# 285

## Pincushions

**Needles cannot rust in a pincushion filled with dried coffee beans.**

# 286

## Seams

Use tweezers to help open a seam. The thread can then be plucked out more easily.

# 287

## Zippers

If a zipper is stuck, rubbing it with a piece of soap will make it open and close easily. To be able to close a zipper at your back without help, lengthen the pull tab by attaching a string with a safety pin.

# 288

## Velvet

To make black velvet as good as new, wipe it with a piece of cloth soaked in kerosene, brush it thoroughly and air well.

# 289

## Socks

To whiten socks discoloured from the insides of shoes, soak them in borax water before washing.

# 290

## Embroidery

Iron embroidered fabrics inside out, placing a piece of cloth soaked in vinegar water between the iron and the embroidery to keep the colour of the delicate fabric fresh.

# 291

## Drying Laundry

If you dry your coloured clothes outside in the summer, turn them inside out so the sun does not bleach them. Adding a pinch of salt to the last rinse cycle keeps the laundry from freezing when hung outside to dry in winter.

# 292

## Fine Washables

Especially sensitive items of clothing will not suffer from a round in the washing machine if they are zipped or buttoned inside a pillow case before being put in the machine.

# 293

## Starching Laundry

Unsalted water from boiling rice is suitable for starching laundry; just sprinkle it onto the clothing when ironing.

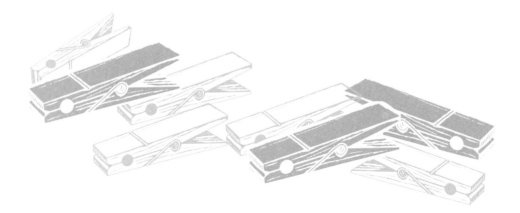

# 294

## Discoloured Laundry

Discoloured laundry can be saved with fresh milk. Soak the laundry in the
milk until the milk sours, then rinse thoroughly with water.

# 295

## Yellowing Fabrics

To prevent yellowing, wrap white fabrics in blue tissue paper, which keeps out damaging sunlight. Fabrics that have already yellowed can be whitened again by rinsing them in a solution of one teaspoon turpentine and one tablespoon alcohol in two and a half gallons of water. You can also soak yellowed fabrics in whole milk for six hours before washing; they will be white again after a normal washing cycle.

# 296

## White Laundry

Adding a package of baking powder with the fabric softener makes whites gleam. Lemon slices added to the wash occasionally also prevent greying.

# 297

## Fabric Softener

Instead of using a commercial fabric softener, add a dash of vinegar to the fabric softener compartment of your washing machine. Vinegar gives a nice scent to the laundry and makes it soft and cuddly. It also protects your washing machine against lime build-up.

# 298

## Shrinking of Wool

Adding some glycerine to the water when washing wool keeps it from shrinking.

# 299

## Compressed Wool

Shrunken wool fabrics that have become compressed like felt become beautiful again when they are soaked overnight in water with hair shampoo. Rinse thoroughly afterwards.

# 300

## Pill Removal

Little pills on your wool fabrics should never be plucked off; they should be cut off cleanly with a small pair of scissors.

# Stains on Clothing

### Orange Juice

To remove orange juice stains, apply some glycerine to the spot and let it soak. Then rinse the garment in lukewarm water.

301

## 302

### Blueberries

Soak blueberry stains in sour milk, and then rinse with lukewarm water.

## 303

### Beer

A beer stain can be washed out with lukewarm water.

# 304

## Pencil

Wash out pencil stains with warm, soapy water. Remove pencil marks from leather fabrics simply by rubbing with a soft eraser.

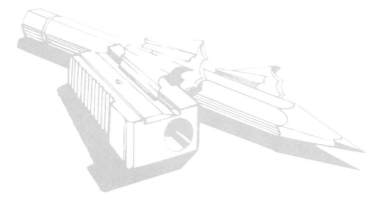

# 305

## Blood

If a bloodstain is still fresh, wash it out with cold water. It is very important that the water be icy cold, because blood clots on contact with warm water, making very persistent stains. Soak dried bloodstains in salt water, rinse the garment in salt water, then finally wash it in warm, soapy water.

## 306

### Wine Cooler

Wine cooler stains can be washed out with soap water. Delicate fabrics can also be treated with diluted ammonia.

## 307

### Butter

Remove butter stains with liquid ammonia.

# 308

## Printing Ink

If printing ink gets on your clothing while you are reading a newspaper,

remove the stain with turpentine.

# 309

## Egg yolk

Egg yolk stains should be treated after they have dried, rather than immediately. Carefully scrape off the top layer by hand, then wash out the rest with benzene.

# 310

## Egg White

Fresh egg white stains can be washed out in cold water. Treat older stains by soaking in diluted ammonia and rinsing in cold water.

# 311

## Strawberries

Wash out fresh strawberry stains with lukewarm water. Older stains disappear in soapy water. With delicate fabrics, dab the stain with pure alcohol, then rinse with water.

# 312

## Putty

**Remove putty stains with turpentine. Soak older stains in turpentine for several hours before removal.**

# 313

## Homemade Stain Remover

Boil haricot beans in unsalted water, then use the water as a gentle but effective stain remover. Unsalted water in which potatoes have been cooked serves the same purpose.

# 314

## Stain Remover for Delicate Fabrics

A dash of liquid ammonia in lukewarm,

soapy water makes a stain remover for delicate fabrics that works well.

# 315

## Stain Remover for Wool

Borax water—a little borax dissolved in boiling water—effectively removes most stains from wool.

# 316

## Grass Stains

A mixture of a dash of alcohol, a few drops of liquid ammonia, and hot water will remove grass stains from most fabrics.

# 317

## Grass on Whites

To treat grass stains in white fabrics, soak the fabric in a solution of ten parts water, ten parts liquid ammonia and one part hydrogen peroxide. Then rinse with cold water.

# 318

Bilberry stains, like blueberry stains, can be treated with sour milk. Soak the stain in it and rinse in warm water.

# 319

## Wood Glue

**Soapy water easily removes wood glue from clothing.**

# 320

## Elderberries

Hydrogen peroxide removes elderberry stains. Be sure to rinse with cold water when the stain is gone.

## 321 Yoghurt

Spilled yoghurt can be brushed away easily after it has dried out.

## 322 Iodine

Rub a fresh iodine stain with a raw potato, then put the item into water; the stain disappears on its own. Treat older stains with a highly diluted ammonia solution.

# 323

## Currant

Fresh currant stains are easily removed by soaking in lemon juice and then rinsing with lukewarm water.

# 324

## Coffee

**Soak coffee stains in glycerine briefly, then simply rinse with water.**

# 325

## Cocoa

Like blood stains, cocoa stains should be washed with cold water first and then with lukewarm water.

## 326

### Lime

**A cloth soaked in vinegar easily removes lime stains.**

## 327

### Chewing Gum

**If you sit on chewing gum, bag the pants in plastic and freeze them until the chewing gum is hard. It will then pull off the fabric easily.**

# 328

## Candle Wax

Put a piece of blotting paper over and under the stain and iron the fabric on the lowest setting. The gentle heat melts the wax, and the blotting paper absorbs it.

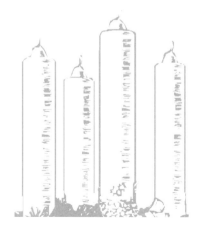

# 329

## Curtains

Yellowed curtains become white again if you add a cup of salt to the soapy water in which they are washed.

## Glue

A remedy against most glues is soaking in alcohol. When the glue is gone,
rinse the area well. For some glues, however, a lukewarm vinegar and
water solution is sufficient.

# 331

## Stewed Fruit

To remove stains made by stewed fruit, first wipe them off with a weak ammonia solution, then soak them overnight in buttermilk with a few dashes of lemon juice. Rinse thoroughly when the stains have disappeared.

# 332

## Ball Point Pen

Bile soap is best for removing the traces of a ballpoint pen. Dab the stain with it, then rinse thoroughly with water. Treat delicate fabrics with pure alcohol. Simple soap water also often works fine for fresh stains.

# 333

## Varnish / Paint

The instructions on the label of varnishes and paints for using turpentine to clean paintbrushes also apply to fabrics. Some paint stains can be treated with alcohol.

# 334

## Liquorice

Remove liquorice stains with liquid ammonia, then rinse thoroughly with water. Liquorice stains can also be washed out with soft soap paste.

# 335

## Liqueur

Liqueur stains can be removed with bile soap. Rinse thoroughly with water afterwards.

# 336

## Lipstick

A generous application of glycerine to lipstick stains makes them disappear in the wash.

# 337

## Jam

**Remove jam stains by first soaking and then washing the article in soapy water.**

# 338

## Machine Oil

If you soak machine oil stains in liquid ammonia, they wash out afterward with lukewarm water.

## Milk

Lukewarm soapy water will take care of fresh milk stains. Older stains disappear when treated with turpentine oil. Rinse the fabric afterwards in water.

# 339

# 340

## Carrots

Apply soft soap paste to carrot stains and soak briefly before washing.

The stain will disappear without a trace.

# 341

## Fruit

**Most fruit stains come out when generously sprinkled with salt (leave it on for a while) before washing.**

# 342

## Perfume

**Glycerine is an effective way to remove perfume stains from most types of fabric.**

# 343

## Kerosene

To remove kerosene stains, sprinkle a lot of cornstarch onto the spots,
cover with blotting paper, and then iron the area with a hot iron.
Afterward, brush off the cornstarch and air the garment outside.

# 344

## Peach

Let peach stains soak well in glycerine, then rinse them with soapy water.

# 345

## Talcum Powder

Brush off as much of the powder as possible, then treat any remaining spots with benzene.

# 346

## Shaving Foam

**Fresh shaving foam stains rinse out easily with warm water. A little vinegar water will remove older stains.**

# 347

## Rust

**Lemon juice easily removes rust stains.**

# 348

## Red Beets

**Rinse red beet stains first with warm soapy water, then remove them with liquid ammonia.**

## 349

### Red Cabbage

Stains from red cabbage can
be washed out with warm
soapy water.

### Red Wine

There is a trick against dreaded red
wine stains as old as it is simple:
Spread a thick layer of salt over the
entire area of the stain and leave it
on for a while,
then wash (or vacuum).

## 350

# 351

## Chocolate

Soak chocolate stains in glycerine, then wash them out with warm soapy water.

## 352 Last Resort Stain Remover

Hold the stained fabric over some boiling water. Drop a small amount of a solution of oxalic acid crystals and water onto the spot, then quickly dip the fabric into the hot water below and rinse thoroughly.

## 353

## Perspiration

Let garments stained by perspiration soak in vinegar water before washing, and the stains will disappear without a trace.

## Mustard

Treat mustard stains with warm soapy water, and then with some liquid ammonia. Briefly soak older stains in glycerine, then wash them out with warm soapy water.

# 355

## Ice Cream

Treat ice cream stains with liquid ammonia mixed with a little soapy water and alcohol. Rinse thoroughly with water afterwards.

## 356

### Grease

For grease stains, sprinkle some cornstarch on the spot and leave it for a while, then brush the cornstarch—and the stains—away.

## 357

### Spinach

Rub spinach stains with a raw potato, then wash them out with lukewarm soap water.

# 358

## Mould Spots

**Before washing clothing with mould spots, soak it overnight in buttermilk with a large dash of vinegar.**

## Tea

Warm soapy water washes out
fresh tea stains. Treat older
stains with glycerine or lemon
juice diluted with water. Rinse
thoroughly in warm water
afterward.

## 360

### Tar

Wash tar stains out first with soapy water, and then treat them
with benzene.

## 361

### Ink

Soak ink stains well in lemon
water, buttermilk, or sour milk
before washing.

# 362

## Tomatoes

Fresh tomato stains can be washed out in soapy water. Soak older stains in soda water before washing.

# Indian Ink

Simply wash out Indian ink stains in cold water.

# 364

## Scorched Stains

Small scorched areas from ironing or a cigarette should be treated immediately. Slice an onion in half and rub the scorched area with the cut surfaces. Leave the onion juice on for a while, then wash in cold water.

# 365

## White Wine

Like red wine stains, white wine stains should be sprinkled liberally
with salt. Then they can be washed out in soapy water.